Walking Our Story

Walking Our Story

Selected and new poems, 2001 to 2016

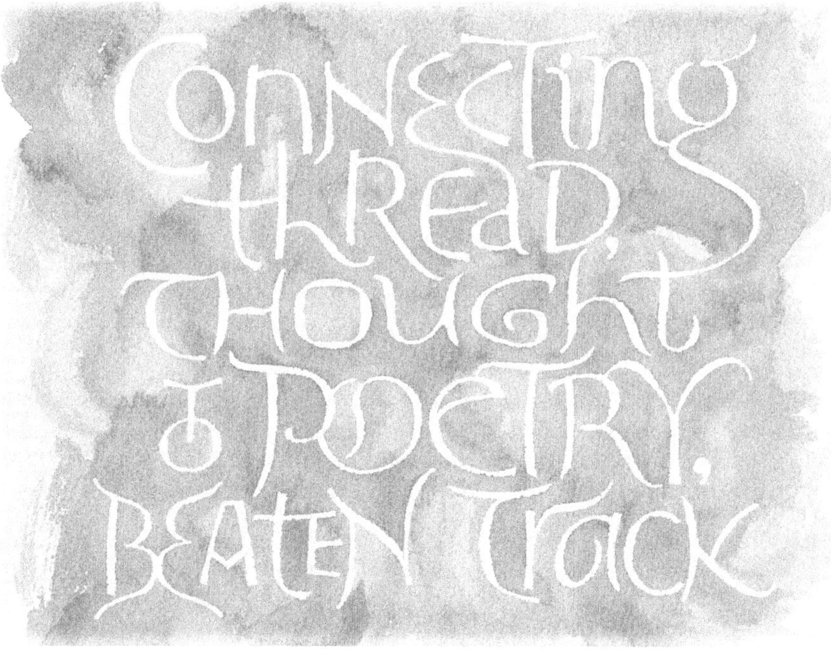

Connecting threads, thoughts & poetry, beaten track

JOY MEAD

wild goose
publications      www.**ionabooks**.com

Content copyright © Joy Mead 2001-2016
Compilation © Joy Mead 2016

First published 2016 by
Wild Goose Publications
21 Carlton Court, Glasgow G5 9JP, UK,
the publishing house of the Iona Community.
Scottish Charity No. SC003794. Limited Company Reg. No. SC096243.

ISBN 978-1-84952-477-3

Cover watercolour by StephenRaw.com

The publishers gratefully acknowledge the support of the Drummond Trust,
3 Pitt Terrace, Stirling FK8 2EY in producing this book.

All rights reserved. Apart from the circumstances described below relating to non-commercial use, no part of this publication may be reproduced in any form or by any means, including photocopying or any information storage or retrieval system, without written permission from the publisher.

Non-commercial use: The material in this book may be used non-commercially for worship and group work without written permission from the publisher. If photocopies of small sections are made, please make full acknowledgement of the source, and report usage to the CLA or other copyright organisation.

Joy Mead has asserted her right in accordance with the Copyright, Designs and Patents Act, 1988, to be identified as the author of this work.

Overseas distribution
Australia: Willow Connection Pty Ltd, Unit 4A, 3–9 Kenneth Road, Manly Vale, NSW 2093
New Zealand: Pleroma, Higginson Street, Otane 4170, Central Hawkes Bay
Canada: Bayard Distribution, 10 Lower Spadina Ave., Suite 400, Toronto, Ontario M5V 2Z

Printed by Bell & Bain, Thornliebank, Glasgow

Contents

Introduction   11
Walking our story   13

From *The One Loaf*, 2001
    The one loaf   16
    Wheat grain   17
    Harvest   18
    Ulva millstones   19
    Out of Egypt   20
    Refugee   21
    Out of the everywhere   22
    Bread-time   24
    Living bread   25
    On the shore   26
    Magnificat now   27
    Pilgrim bread   28

From *A Telling Place*, 2002
    Faith mother   32
    Women at the well   33
    Apple life   34
    Woman without a name   35
    Rachel   36
    Scarlet women   37
    Sisera's mother   38
    Orpah   39
    Miriam's song   41
    Blooming women   42
    Waiting   43

Mary's song   44
Wise women   44
Jairus' daughter   46
Gethsemane   47
The women see ...   48
In the margins   49

From *Where Are the Altars*, 2007

Things   52
Speaking peace   54
Well-being   55
Empty shoes   56
Grass snake   58
Sheepfolds   59
In Regents Park   60
Sheela-na-gig at Kilvickeon   61
Sir, you have no bucket ... and the well is deep   62
Mary   64
An ordinary miracle   65
Resurrection   67
Living in the cracks   68
Refugees   70
Palimpsest   70
Wedding song   71
Corncrake   72
Elemental   73
Apples   74
The seven colours of imagination   75
   Iona rainbow   75
   Red   75
   Orange   77

Contents

Introduction   11
Walking our story   13

From *The One Loaf*, 2001

    The one loaf   16
    Wheat grain   17
    Harvest   18
    Ulva millstones   19
    Out of Egypt   20
    Refugee   21
    Out of the everywhere   22
    Bread-time   24
    Living bread   25
    On the shore   26
    Magnificat now   27
    Pilgrim bread   28

From *A Telling Place*, 2002

    Faith mother   32
    Women at the well   33
    Apple life   34
    Woman without a name   35
    Rachel   36
    Scarlet women   37
    Sisera's mother   38
    Orpah   39
    Miriam's song   41
    Blooming women   42
    Waiting   43

Mary's song   44
Wise women   44
Jairus' daughter   46
Gethsemane   47
The women see ...   48
In the margins   49

From *Where Are the Altars*, 2007

Things   52
Speaking peace   54
Well-being   55
Empty shoes   56
Grass snake   58
Sheepfolds   59
In Regents Park   60
Sheela-na-gig at Kilvickeon   61
Sir, you have no bucket ... and the well is deep   62
Mary   64
An ordinary miracle   65
Resurrection   67
Living in the cracks   68
Refugees   70
Palimpsest   70
Wedding song   71
Corncrake   72
Elemental   73
Apples   74
The seven colours of imagination   75
   Iona rainbow   75
   Red   75
   Orange   77

Yellow   79
Green   80
Blue   82
Indigo   83
Violet   84

From *Words and Wonderings*, 2011

The words and wonderings of being alive   88
Might it be called wisdom?   89
Bread poetry   89
If   90
Pomegranates   92
What I know about orchards …   93
Conversation   94
A dream of markets …   94
The seas of Kirk Swarf   95
Symphony   97
Waiting for an artist   97
A poem to saunter with …   98
The music of humanity   99
In a notebook   100
A spider called Spurious   101
Communing   102
Hope: a moment of being   103
The fire, the circle, the listening, the talking   104
In the garden   105
The story   106

From *A Way of Knowing*, 2012

A way of knowing   108
Poetry   109

Wild places 110
What I know about Orkney is that … 110
Scissors 112
Hanging out the words 113
The boat 114
A grain of sand 115
What I know about flowers 117
Poet in the gallery 118
String Trio, Peter Maxwell Davies 120
Ordinary, particular, universal 121

From *Glimpsed in Passing*, 2014

Today 124
Wool, wood, stone 127
A grey day 128
Alone 128
Big words 129
A photograph of birdsong? 130
The gate 131
Glimpsed in passing 132
To imagine … 134
I do not know God 135
A time to walk … and a time to stand … 138
On the earth 140
A workaday fiddle 141
'The sea wants to be visited' 142
'A few … may creep back, silent' 143
Abiding (2) 145
Golden Wedding 146
The road home 147

New poems 2015/16

A parable of being   150
Re-reading Middlemarch at 70   151
Last leaves   152
Knitting pattern   154
Thoughts on doing nothing …   156
Housekeeping   157
The ways of the world … thoughts in a doctors' waiting room   158
Spring haiku   160
Summer haiku   160
Autumn haiku   161
Winter haiku   161
Bowl   162
To laugh   163
If I am ever thankful   164
History   165
Shoreline   166
Thoughts too deep?   167
Withdrawn   168
Christmas card angel   170
At the Broch of Gurness   171
From the edge …   173
Emptiness   174
To be called Joy   175

Introduction

I hope this collection will be enjoyable and useful. It is something of the story of my own walk through life and inevitably tells of love and friendship. So I hope it will be of use to those friends who ask me 'Where can I find … ?' when they want a poem for a particular occasion. With them in mind I have tried to select the poems I've been asked about most (which are not necessarily amongst the best ones!) as well as some of the most telling favourites.

My thanks to all at Wild Goose Publications and especially to Sandra for her kindness, support, encouragement and efficient handling of written material; to Steve Raw for another beautiful cover; to Ian and our family and many dear friends who walk with me … and to the strangers I meet in unexpected but blessed encounters along the way.

The walk, the story, the poetry, go on …

Joy Mead,
April, 2016

Walking our story

On footpaths, green lanes
and holloways,

harrowed paths, sunken roads,
drove roads to market,
ways to church,
pilgrim paths,

the way to the sea.

Connecting thread,
thought to poetry,
beaten track:
our paths, settled ways,
without impulse
or suddenness,
are mysterious
and humbling.
They tell of tendency,
of desire, of loving.

A life of journeys,
an archive of paths
trodden by innumerable feet.

The feeling intelligence,
the way to the undiscovered,
the way home.

from
The One Loaf
2001

The one loaf

Out of fire
its bodily contours
satisfying to all senses:
a warm loaf; seedy, grainy
soft and being-shaped,
its yeasty smell, homely
and heavenly, of fungus
and damp autumn woodlands
… and the sun's warmth.

All life is here:
ordinary, good, beautiful:
growing things and cow dung,
woody roots and seeds,
bodies of creatures
long dead in the soil;
all in this given bread
of our beginnings;
all in breaking
and sharing
our one loaf.

Wheat grain

The given beauty of it –
inert in my palm
tender, fragile thing
quietly holding
good for all people,
complex and intricate,
storing life and the means
of life.

The silent wonder of it –
Jack and the beanstalk story:
always ready to sprout
while the sower is away;
fairy story; or miracle:
seed, soil, labour, love;
life, death, rebirth,
earth's best gift,
seed of freedom
for all our tomorrows.

Harvest

Those who sow in tears
will reap with songs of joy.
He who goes out weeping
carrying his bag of seed
will come back with songs of joy
carrying home his sheaves.
(Psalm 126)

Waving wheat
and dancing feet;
wooing of earth,
gathering grain
and people;
bringing home sheaves
with music and laughter
gathering time
and memory.

Lugh, god of harvest-time,
sits so lightly to life
he has been known
to dance on a bubble
without bursting it.

His celebration
is music and movement,
rhythm of seasons;
sowing and harvest;

wordless; fragile
as a bubble:
yet as enduring
as the heart
of uncrushable joy.*

* Lughnasa, the festival of Lugh, the Celtic God of the Harvest, was so important in the lives of the people of Ireland and so involved with their ideas of welfare that Christianity had to adopt it or permit it to survive.

Ulva millstones

On the far shore of an island
where to look is healing,
I pause
sensing that I have arrived;
looking for somewhere to rest
my eyes.

At my feet
disused and discarded
are two massive millstones,
moss-covered, almost hidden,
cradled in nettles,
perfectly at home.

They guard the essence
of their story
circling the unsaid
centre which is sustenance
in this place of regeneration
where there are ghosts
of bread.

Out of Egypt
(Numbers 11:8)

When Moses led the Israelite slaves
out of Egypt, the women
took their millstones
not as a weight
around their necks
but as heart and hearth
of home: the means
to make the manna
of their dreams
into the bread
of life.

Refugee

Roasted grains offered
into open hands:
water shared; bread broken
... in harmony with each other
and with God's good earth
which fed them all
in this man's
fertile land.

She had come from afar
seeking this place of refuge,
carrying her own suffering,
her hunger ... and her story
deep inside her.

'Why' she asked the good man
from Bethlehem
'are you so kind
as to notice me
a stranger in your land.'

'Come' he said 'I have heard
your story; you are stranger
no longer; come and eat
the fruit of my fields.
There is bread between us.'

Story in her;
story in him;
difference joyfully shared,
... pieces picked up
like broken grain
and kneaded gently
to make a new story
to change the world.

Out of the everywhere
(Matthew 13:33)

In the beginning
is the yeast.
This quietest of all possibilities
lives on leaves and tree bark,
in soil and on fruit skins,
in seed and fresh air,
comes from the everywhere.

A woman, the storyteller
of long ago Palestine
tells us, takes this yeast,
and adds to it
three measures of flour.
Tended by time

and a woman's caring
hands, the yeast begins
its all pervasive activity.
Quietly, gently, it renews,
enlarges, transforms,
irreversibly filling all matter
with anticipation and airiness,
with creative, life-affirming
vitality.

The storyteller sits butterfly light
to life. He makes water into wine
to give the party sweetness
and flavour. He celebrates
the beauty of bread;
pictures its sensual
sculptural, visual pleasure;
touches the moment
when the prospect of a hard grain cake
becomes the possibility
that satisfies
belly, spirit and senses:
the full-bodied
breadiness of bread: purity
in wholeness and joy:
the livingness of life.

And the yeast
holds on to its mystery.

Bread-time

1
Because bread won't be hurried
we have to learn to let be,
to do nothing, to be patient,
to wait for the proving.
Because bread won't be hurried
and is a life and death process,
we find out in its making
that time is not a line
but a cycle of ends and beginnings
rhythms and seasons,
growth and death,
celebration and mourning
work and rest,
eating and fasting,
because bread won't be hurried.

2
In a pyramid in Egypt
a few grains of wheat
lay surrounded by death:
dormant for thousands of years.
They waited quietly
until the time was right,
until the life impulse
was awakened by the good earth,

warmed by the sun
and ready to dance
in the bread of tomorrow.

Living bread

Knowing bread
is knowing the whole round
of life – shaped
from wood and roots,
bodies of dead animals,
peat and grass,
water and honey sweetness:
the best of earth's gifts
shaped into fleshiness,
so that we wonder
at its softness:
how it smells like us
salty and moist, good
for one last deathlike gesture:
oven burial, home to warmth.

Then joy in the rising,
the finished loaf
and our own becoming.

We are what we eat.

On the shore

Wind is fresh on his face,
water laps at his feet,
a fire is ready
for the fish and bread meal
at the heart of his story.
Alone, he waits on the shore
for the fishers to come.

And they, with a catch
heavier than their dreams,
sail wondering into this story.
His greeting has the wholeness
of bread and poetry.
No word to suggest dogma or creed;
no ninety-nine impossible things
to believe before breakfast
but this one thing:
life ... in all its abundance
... to be savoured and shared:
'Come and have breakfast'

John 21:9-14

Magnificat now
(for Bob Holman)

The birthing of the ordinary
revolution: women's voices
sound Magnificat
making an enormous YES

on housing estates
and travellers' sites,
in hostels for the homeless
and cardboard cities;

in community food shops,
credit unions,
soup kitchens
and baby co-ops;

where the rhythm of a song
moves the people's dreams
like flowers scattered
at the site of a stabbing;

where the handmaid
of the Lord, in her own
shaft of light
stands tall and empowered
breaking each day
in community
the 25p sliced bread
of life.

Pilgrim bread

Touch tenderly: earth, water, air,
salt, time and broken grain –
this one life
in all. Touch
with loving hands;

hands to make
to shape and mould,
warm, moisty dough,
feeling fleshy,
smelling earthy;

hands to bake,
well crusted bread
set by the sun,
transformed by fire,
warm with wonder;

hands to break
and break again
pilgrim bread
for pilgrim people.

In the kitchens,
from the tables,
priests of the moment
we dare to serve
this quiet mystery
this risen life,
gift of the earth,
gift of our hands,
for all to share.

from
A Telling Place
Reflections on the stories of women in the Bible
2002

Faith mother

I feel your nearness more acutely now
old woman: the last to be freed
from cruel joke and mocking cliché.

No longer put to death as witch
but often confined as confused.
Your seeing is threatening

(at menopause they say
women often see the devil)

and stands in the way
of conformity to a pattern
in which the human body is beautiful
only if it is young, shapely
and smells good.

But like Sarah long ago
you can still laugh
at the overlarge egos
of old men
hungry for lost dreams.

Your inner beauty
is the mysterious wisdom
of a heart, as yet, unbowed.
Your long and earthy memory
holds the experience of ages
of seeing and being

of waiting and pondering
all things in your heart.

Your ancient understanding
could even now be our hope
and our salvation.

Women at the well

Thirsty people, wanting
containers for their needs
and their longings;
women with the means
to draw fresh water;
colour, activity
fertile wetness,
bodies of hope –
gather around a possibility
of blossoming deserts
and flourishing people;
growing food
and healthy children.

A well is a telling place
where perceptions are changed
and tomorrow reshaped;
where hidden stories
bubble up joyfully

to heal and enliven
every part
of our shared being.

Apple life

She wants to bite.
This small globe –
the unforgettable apple –
holds the colours
of an autumn hillside,
the sunlight glow
of long summer days;
an earthy ripeness,
a tongue-tingling sharp sweetness,
luscious wetness and cool crispness:
the taste of Eden.

Just one bite explodes in her mouth.
Is it too much to want
knowledge and the garden,
sweetness and ashes?
She sees the fruit fall,
the ripe seed die
in the ground
so that tomorrow
the air may be filled
with the heady scent
of apple blossom.

Woman without a name
Judges 19

Woman
without a name,
raped and abused
until break of day
then taken limb by limb
through the length of the land.
What symbolism is this?
What do I hear
in your silences?

Who questions your abuse
and the crime
against female sexuality,
when the only question is misuse
of man's property?

Can I stand in solidarity
with your pain
and let the silence be
wordless?

Is your silence
louder than the cry
from the cross?

Rachel
(Genesis 29-35)

Some way from the angels
of Bethel, Ben-oni's longed-for birth
takes Rachel's breath away.
Bargaining for mandrakes,
concealing household gods,
uneasy dreaming
all move into
emptiness.

A silent memory
holds true –
Rachel becomes her Self:
all breath, pure colour;
dappled, brindled, spotted:
angel-light of our imaginings:
shaped in sheep and goats
 – named for the angel-tracker
Jacob's love
of his dark and beautiful bride;
 – woven for ever
into the multicoloured story
of Joseph's unforgettable coat.

Scarlet women

Red ribbons or cords –
bookmarks in the pages
of history;
writing in the margins,
surprise or warning,
alerting me to interruptions
in a genealogy.

Now I see
women's hands reach out,
tears stain the pages.
I hear cries echoing
from a far place.

I begin to wonder
about the missing stories.
What would they tell,
these free and generous beings
who are all things to all men?

Tamar and Rahab –
prostituted for a storyteller's pleasure,
manipulated to show the hand
of history,
manhandled to proclaim
the greatness of Israel's God

and his guidance
at their cost
at all cost.

Tamar, we are told in Genesis 38, pretends to be a prostitute; Rahab, who features in Joshua 2, is a prostitute. Neither tells her own story nor is it told by another. The storyteller uses them, takes his pleasure of both and when they are no longer needed (for theological purposes) he discards them and we hear no more until surprisingly they reappear in the genealogy of Jesus in the first chapter of Matthew's Gospel.

Sisera's mother
(Judges 5)

Who does not cast a glance
to where an unnamed mother sits
silently, at the edge of her story?

Pondering in her heart
the things of his growing, she waits,
powerless and voiceless,
for the hoofbeat of his horses
on the soil of home;
while talk is of damsels
and dyed stuff
to grace a victor's neck.

She watches the dawning:
the gradual revealing
of a vast emptiness,
for many share the dying
but few the knowing.

The rays of the morning sun
pierce her heart
and her still body is the shape
of a multitude of grieving women;
for no one asks the mothers
when the talk is of war
and the spoils of war.

Orpah

The necessary pots and pans
weigh heavy on her back
as she travels far out
towards a country
she knows nothing about.

The story is ambivalent:
choice and no choice,
first this way
then the other way
showing the back of her neck

to Naomi and Ruth –
as if this is all
there is to tell.
She goes back to her own people
and her mother's house

to affirm self and community
in Moabite traditions.
Here she shares memories
and the retelling of sacred stories:
her people's beginnings
in fertile valleys –
farming and fruit
and food for the feast
in Sodom and Gomorrah;
earthquakes and active volcanoes;
pillars of salt and people
named for their strength
to survive a disaster.

Orpah, princess
in her own country,
dreaming of Ruth,
Moabite stranger
in another land,
awaits images
adequate for her own telling –
knowing that everyone must live
her own beautiful story.

Miriam's song
(Exodus 15:19-21)

Miriam singing; Miriam dancing;
Miriam wonderer
walking on air.

Miriam laughing; Miriam crying;
Miriam wanderer
walking on earth.

Miriam watching; Miriam minding;
Miriam prophetess:
crafting her story.

Stepping out lightly
pulsing with beauty;
wise and far seeing,
going before us;

Trusting the dance,
willing and dreaming;
filling us all
with the music of hope.

Blooming women

At the garden's edge
I see the waiting women
of all time.

From the margin of history
they put the buds
of their silence
into my hands
outstretched from the future.

And the flowers that open
are vibrant and outrageous
blooming with all the colours
of a new centre of being
which is my body
and my surprise.

Waiting

Somewhere between Annunciation
and Magnificat,
between the angel thought
and the setting out
into the unknown,
is the waiting time

when ordinary happenings:
  leaping of babies,
  conversations of home,
  holding out hands,
  in friendship and trust,
become miracles
that bridge the gap
between loving and being

then the words that tumble out
of the everyday
begin to take the rhythm
of a liberation song
and the body moves wholly
towards tomorrow.

Mary's song
(Luke 1)

Mary, earthy mother,
common woman:
you sing to your son
songs that will move hearts
to change the world, if only
we learn to listen
and delve to the deep
human source
of your heavenly music.

Wise women

Nobody saw them go
– those men of the world
we fondly call wise.
They came laden with gifts
but with little to share –
kept their distance,
and left quietly
by a different route.

Back home, satisfied
that they understand

the meaning of pilgrimage
and well out of the way
of the innocents' cries,
they talk of their experiences,
feel themselves born again.

Far beyond the reach of their thinking
the morning sun touches the quiet stable
with a new day's warmth.
Women come from Bethlehem town
carrying bread freshly baked
in the star-studded night.
They come, as at every birth:
to wonder at tiny fingers and toes,
to welcome holy flesh and blood,
with the joy of touch and kiss and story,
to look deep into innocent
infant eyes, and ponder
'What will this child be?'

The women share the bread
with resurrection laughter
and moisten its earthiness
with everlasting tears –
for unnumbered nameless children die today
and the sound of Rachel's weeping
is never far away.

Jairus' daughter
(Mark 5:35-43)

'Get up, my child!'
This is no time for sleeping.
Lighter than Lazarus,
this raising; his touch
an affirmation of womanhood
amid the misted familiar.

Flute players retune
to celebrate the coming
of her bleeding, and the chance,
between waxing and waning
of moons, for new life.

Mother and father watch,
unable to do anything
but offer wholesome food
for the journey.
The threshold is hers
to cross alone; her knowing
is outside theirs
in the shadow of the unsaid.

Gethsemane

At Gethsemane the skirts of light
grow wider in the immense dark,
revealing watchers at the gate.*

The women there – watching, seeing,
awake: waiting without interfering,
quiet in their humble love.

While sleeping men no longer attend,
the women focus wholly
on the depths of human experience.

Helpless, baffled, marginalised,
with a precious generosity
they minister with eyes and ears.

They are waiting with patient attention
for the insight not yet given;
waiting and never relinquishing

the ability to feel; never losing
the capacity for compassion
or the strength to hope;

waiting and holding on to their vision;
forever at the gate;
forever ready.

Legend tells that while the apostles slept in the Garden of Gethsemane (Matthew 26:38) when Jesus had asked them to stay awake and pray, Mary and Martha were awake, watching and praying at the Garden gate.

The women see …
(Mark 16)

Stone is heavy with the weight
of nothing:
there at the beginning;
there when Mary comes early
to the tomb
and sees the emptiness
containing everything;

sees the morning rays
of a rising sun;
light and shadow
on each blade
of new grown grass,
fragile, transient, moving
with the weight
of eternity and endless
crucifixion.

Nothing to hold;
nothing to know.
Only the surprise
and the communion:
butterfly and bird,
her flowing tears,
love without condition
and a shout of joy.

In the margins

Shadows of unknowing
pattern the pages.
Pencil ponderings
underline, make quiet
announcements – a word here
a paragraph there.
Insights search
for images.

Cherished connections
are gently made
from the marks
of our humanness:

finger prints,
a smudge of blood,
the stain of a tear.
Another story
rests in these interruptions ...

like Hagar in the wilderness
waiting;
Miriam by the sea
dancing;
Mary in the stable
wondering
after the visitors leave.

Back in the ordinary place
somewhere in the margins
of history –
in the kitchen, maybe –
annunciation is always
happening.

from
Where Are the Altars?
2007

Things

In this room
I breathe words.
Things with one another
make a story:

books on ledge and shelf
on desk and floor
... books on books,
a 'book chair' I never use,
poems on postcards,
an invitation to an authors' party –
I can't go;

a medieval allegory of the scribe's tools
to remind me of the responsibility of words;

photographs of William, Alasdair,
Emily and Oliver
to remind me of tomorrow,

a key from a piano
that once made music
in Iona Abbey,
stones from St Columba's Bay
that still shout aloud;

a framed strawberry,
a large cut-out Tigger,
a sparkly apple,
paper flowers from a 'Blooming Women Day'
long ago in Manchester,
a bunch of cut-out cardboard cornflowers
from Catherine and Andrew's wedding day;

a silver spoon from Glasgow University,
a cross from Peru,
peace poppies on a string,
a waving ladybird clock –
Catherine says 'Every home should have one' –
a papier-mâché penguin
the children next door made for me,
a 'Mouseman' book rack;

a dream catcher – complete with invisible dreams,
the 'Growing hope' collage Jan made for me
 in 1995 – the year I had cancer,
the empty John Leach bowl Ian gave me
which fits perfectly in my open hands.

Speaking peace
(Fionnphort 2002)

There are stories in the wind today.
I breathe the language of a field
heady with the scent of midsummer
meadowsweet: favourite flower
to honey the mead,
strew rooms with sweetness
that makes hearts glad.
Cuchulainn*, long ago hero,
rode out, we are told,
with the creamy blossoms
in his belt to cool his rage.

And exuberant loosestrife,
that patterns the same meadow
with ripples the colour
of purple red passion,
once calmed ox and horse
yoked together.

*Legendary Irish hero whose violent story is told in The Ulster Cycle

Well-being

There is blessing
in things that matter, together:

the quiver of joy each year
when the first daffodil opens,
the way a sightless dying man touches
a young girl's engagement ring –
and remembers his long-dead love,
Iona dawn – the light
on my face – and knowing
this is the place to be,
looking into the faces
of friends
in a crowded teashop,
the way cotton grass
catches both wind and sun,
daisies and dandelions that come
from nowhere,
stillness held in an empty bowl
and the hands around it,
a child who puts a hand
in mine telling me
there is tomorrow,
the spring blossom,
bee-filled, tongue-tingling promise
of an apple,
an elderly Sikh

early one morning in High Wycombe
carrying a sheaf of gladioli,
fragile threads of chance
that make encounters
into friendships,
the barely perceptible
and never-to-be held moment
when the eyes that see
and the wild rose that is seen
are one.

Empty shoes

A pair of gold strappy sandals,
worn down by dancing and treading lightly
on daisied lawns at dawn,
disturbed in the dust
of an old woman's wardrobe;
one baby shoe tied to the fence
of an army base;
dirty trainers in a teenager's bedroom;
one boot washed up on a riverbank;
shoes left at the door of a mosque;

the shoes Daley Thompson
took from the feet of Kelly Holmes
after she won the Olympic gold;
the sandals by the sea that remind me
of school corridors
and endless summertime.

Unworn shoes float away in a flood;
shoes of bomb victims
lie scattered in a road;
rows of unneeded shoes wait
in the wardrobes of the powerful
after their downfall;
shoes fill a tree in a park
with stories – like souls after death –
hanging unclaimed.

Shoes, telling of holy ground
they once walked on.

Grass snake

Olive-grey coil
of stillness, head up
orange collar
catching the sun,
watching

becomes
in a moment
all movement,
flowing like warm oil
into the grass.

The wonder could be
it comes so close
to where we sit

and yet I think
the wonder
is to look at it.

Tonight there may be stars
here in the same way
as the snake is here
and has always known
something.

Sheepfolds
(John 10:6-9)

I love the shape of the fold:
the bowl-like roundness of stones
moulded one into another,
holding fast. Each one pulls
into the whole,
each one bears witness
to the memory
of human and animal.
Andy Goldsworthy, I think,
is some sort of shepherd.

Stones together intensify space
quietly: enfold a holy emptiness:
space for imagination
and children's play,
ground for circles, cycles, curves,
ends that are always beginnings.

The story tells of a shepherd
who made his body a door.
We still love the shape
of the words
that keep us safe
and bring us home.

In Regents Park
28th September, 2006
(For Margaret with love)

Summer's last roses
bloom late this year
and their petals blow
strange patterns across
the path of coming winter.

Shall we think that somewhere
in this weary world
old women are getting up
at dawn each day to queue
for bread to feed the children?

Shall we look for words
to grow old in, poetry
for the grief of the world

or shall we be extravagant
with the morning, pause
to smell the roses,
let the language
of scent and colour,
the hush of friendship,
be enough for today?

Sheela-na-gig at Kilvickeon *

We might easily miss it:
high on the east wall.

Some say it's a warning about lust
but I like to think it mouths a 'yes'
to birth and beginnings.

There's no evil here –
the devil, they say, can't stand
the sight of a woman's sex.

This is a place of storied light,
where angel questions
hang in the air;
a layered place
where we might hear
in the silence
the intimate murmurs
of the unremembered
who lie deeper
than the marked graves.

A story is being told
in language just beyond
our reach.
So don't use the word 'god' –

or even 'goddess' –
unless you hear
the rumour.

* A sheela-na-gig is a carving of a woman with exposed and sometimes exaggerated genitalia found on religious buildings. Kilvickeon is a ruined 13th-century chapel and burial ground, near Scoor on the Ross of Mull.

Sir, you have no bucket … and the well is deep
(John 4:11)

The clanking sound of an empty bucket
echoes like an elaborate theory
that makes devastating sense.

But what makes the sad world lovely
is that somewhere it hides a wellspring
without a bucket.

We may never find the well
but our thirst will be satisfied
by the search, the coming close
and wondering:
does the one know
and the other feel
or are the knowing

and the feeling
together in the flow
that carries the pain
and the joy of the world?

Weep over injustice,
rejoice in goodness,
love outrageously.

Let uncertainty
flow on the stillness
of our bodies
and the story be told
in freshly drawn water.

Sir, you have no bucket, and the well is deep (John 4:11) is one of my favourite Bible verses. The poem looks at our attempt and desire to hold life within elaborate theories/theologies which are often devastating to wholeness. Whereas embodied thinking means we can't detach ourselves from how what we do, or decide, feels – for us and others. We carry the pain of the world on our bodies (what the whole Jesus story is about surely?). If you separate mind and body you can rationalise any atrocity.

I feel that the woman at the well story shows us a lot about accompaniment, giving out of what we do not have and the flowing together of heart and mind.

Mary
(John 12:1-8)

Luxurious loving released
in the pouring out
of sweet-scented oil:
essence that defines her love,
marks a soaring vision,

a moment of awakening,
the alchemy of imagination
heightened colour, sound, movement,
in soft womanliness, the evanescence
of life and quiet grace;
free-flowing hair,
a body of fire
and a mind
on a journey,

beauty remembered for ever
and enough to carry hope
to a broken world.

An ordinary miracle
(For Christopher on St Andrew's Day 2000)

The first to come out of the crowd
as the sun goes down:
a small guardian of the future
with trust in his eyes
and hope in his hands.

In him, Andrew sees something
of himself; meets a memory:
a shadow of long ago when he was a boy,
his energy unsullied and his vision clear;
a whisper from the depths of his being
about fairness and sharing
and simple answers.

A disciple in an impossible position,
reminded of his first care –
to feed others,
wondering about miracles;
a boy bearing food, risking ridicule,
trusting the bread of life:
here, now, late in the day
they make their way
to one whose work
is in such small but costly acts;
who sees in each hungry face
an essential fragility,

a childlike joy
not wholly lost
to a bigger future.

And so …
in this once upon a time moment …
the story begins.
Outrageous hope, outspoken love,
are released like nudging angels
amongst people longing
for comfort and community,
sensing the beginnings of friendships.

Child, disciple and the one who understands
just and equal sharing:
know there will be enough
to go round;
refuse to say 'It can't be done.'

So it happens – the great feast:
hearts and hands, baskets and pockets,
open;
neighbour gives bread
and peace to neighbour,
each makes a place for another
and in this most ordinary of miracles
all are fed.

Resurrection ...

All the way home
that autumn day
he talked about leaves.
He had watched
them come down,
picked up one or two,
looked at them sadly:
'The trees are broken ...' he said
and tried to put the leaves back
on the lower branches
just within his reach.

'No,' we said 'they don't fit back.
The tree will sleep now. In spring
the leaves will come again.'

Beginnings of a smile ...
then he ran among the fallen leaves,
enjoying the sound,
learning how things
are meant to be.

An April day – a few clouds
in a blue sky,
a hint of warmth
in the air, softness
and the feeling

that something new
is just beginning.

William, glad to be out,
looks up at the trees,
sees the first signs
of leaves and cries out
'The spring did it!'

Living in the cracks

Ivy-leaved Toadflax ...
... a name that gives nothing
away – almost a disguise

to cover the tales
other names tell:
Travelling Sailor,
(come a long journey)
Mother of Thousands
(giving birth to stories)
Madonna's Flower
(looking to the angels).

Seeds came in secretly
centuries ago, hidden in the cracks
of marble figures from Italy.

Migrant, refugee, stranger –
not knowing how to go wild
with the yellow Common Toadflax
that dances in waste places,
you developed a liking for domestic walls,
embedded yourself in Cotswold stone
and became the Oxford Weed.

Then when the time was right,
your offspring travelled secretly

to the edges,

to the walls of the Abbey
on Iona where a cascade of flowers
touches my bare legs
like the hands of forgotten children

or to become, on Yeats' tower,
like poetry: a conversation
that connects, an interruption,
tentative, maybe, but big enough

to fill the cracks of our domesticity
and colour our broken places.
Part of the scene; here to stay.

Refugees

A place like a pause,
an interruption, where seeds
lay, undying.

The air is light and empty,
the cottage long gone
in the process
of building and razing
communities.

Poppies and marigolds,
way of life and death plants
emerge, like a conversation
I've never had
yet might hold
in my open hands.

Palimpsest

It almost ceases to be
a gravestone

and becomes a secret
garden, a timeless memorial
to hiddenness.

Rain runs down
in runnels like rivers
through a many-coloured land
of strange trees.
Water is carving
its own story,
making another layer
of meaning
over writing
we can no longer see.

Wedding song
(for Catherine and Andrew)

As if the beautiful future
is here in the joyful now
dance, dance
for this wedding day,
swing, swing
in the rhythm of life
that follows the one
who makes the pure water
flow like honey-sweet wine,
the gift of hope,
the best for last.

Follow the one
with a sackful of wings
to lift us off our feet
in starburst
colourburst
flowerburst.

Today is the world's beginning,
today every word
turns to poetry,
today is our dancing day.

Corncrake
(Matthew 6:33)

Nutty noise-maker,
most enigmatic of birds,

almost a name
for the unfound
and unseen,

for points of reference
that keep moving about.

You could watch the field
all day and never see it.

There is only that sound
like an angel's laugh
telling us
we're always close
never there.

Elemental

When my time is over
and fire has consumed
all flesh, take my dust
and scatter it
where you can feel
earth, water, rushing air
that I may be
whole.

Then take away with you
memories, burning in fire,
fresh as air, rolling as the sea,
still as the earth
and this shall be
my resurrection.

Apples

I have a sort of dream
of a hidden orchard and the soft air
of a late summer evening.
Butterflies feast on fallen fruit.

In the fading light, I reach up
and hold an apple
in my hand.
It rests there
against the stars
just visible
through the branches.

I smell its sharp-sweet flesh,
sense its mystery.

I'm holding life and legends
in one hand.

Apples were there at the beginning
before words,
before they took their place
in story.

Inside this red-gold globe
are tiny storehouses for the heady scent
of orchards in full bloom
and the flowering of human dreams.

Once monks were buried in orchards.
Imagine a graveyard in blossom time.
How could you not believe
in resurrection?

The seven colours of imagination

Iona rainbow

The rainbow
arching the Abbey now
is like a thin air bridge
between the stones on the shore
and eternity
with no meaning
but poetry.

Red

is the smell
of strawberries
on a summer evening

and warm earth
beneath bare feet.

Reaching out red
is the unsettling sound
of a song of longing.

Red is wind on the hill
and the hot blast
of a trumpet.

Like peppers and pimentos,
it's the colour of fire
and warning: be careful
you might get burnt.

Red is the stop and look
powdered pigment of Anish Kapoor,
Wassily Kandinsky's radiant brush strokes,
Chagall's angel and one of Franz Marc's horses:
the lively one (the quiet one is blue);
and Andy Goldsworthy's poppy petals
wrapped round a hazel branch.

Ochres from the earth
run blood red when wet
and madder is the rhythm
of the rubia tree roots.

Red is raw; red is birth.
Red is spilt blood.

Disturbed earth bleeds poppies.

Red I think
might be the colour of God

Orange

You bring a gift
of clementines – almost
from Palestine
where, you tell,
2000 years of care
for land and ancient trees
brings a plentiful harvest.

We sing and cry and dance and laugh
the glowing orange warmth
of hope

and warning:
eye-catching orange paints
dangerous parts of machinery.

'Orange,' Kandinsky said,
'is like a man convinced
of his own powers'

or a woman maybe
with a basket of fruit
in Drury Lane.

Brian Keenan was persuaded
by the colour orange
that he would survive.

The robes of Buddhist monks
glow in orange contrast
to the plain wooden bowls
in their hands.

Orange is the settled background
of Winifred Nicholson's
Honeysuckle and Sweetpeas

and something disturbing
in Van Gogh's sunflowers.

It's the lump
in the end of a stocking
on Christmas morning,

the smell of luxury,
a reminder of poverty.

Orange is the varnish
Stradivari used,
the sound of a violin
playing in the rain

and a bunch of marigolds
on an unmarked grave.

Yellow

is the silent yes
of a field full of buttercups
and the sound of a harp playing
in the first warmth of the morning.

It's the feel of dry grass
on bare ankles,
brimstone butterflies against sky blue
and a garden loud with bees,
the smell of haymaking
and a field of wheat grain waiting.

Yellow is the colour of kindness,
amber, honey, saffron,
the oily taste of sunflower seeds,
eggs, butter, Easter morning
and how the blackbird's beak
resists the dark.

It's the glowing beard
of Chagall's *Jew in Green*
and the elm leaves
that Andy Goldsworthy
laid over a rock
at low water in Dumfriesshire.

Yellow is fear, jaundice
and blisters on tired feet;

old documents, letters,
and newspapers
at the bottom of a drawer;

sand through an hourglass
and over-wintered apples.

It's chrysanthemums laid on a coffin,
and a light in a distant window.

Green

is the earth's holding
of river, pond and lake,
the way the hills roll
towards the water,
a many-shaded landscape.

It's tenderness and generosity
lavish, yet spreading itself lightly
with something saved
for tomorrow.

Green is a child's first words,
the side of the apple
that isn't blushing
and the sea where it isn't blue.

Green sounds like a rippling river,
and soft wind in the trees,

smells like the wet grass
on a spring morning.

It's peppermint ice cream
the woodpecker's back,
the gloss on a mallard

and Georgia O'Keefe's
vibrant oak leaves.

Green is the colour my mother wears
in a black and white photograph.

It's the other side of the fence,
jealousy, envy, pus, infection
the colour eggs go,
and a bruise as it heals.

Green is bendy and pliable,
what I want to hold on to
in old age

I think the other side of death
might be green.

Blue

is a Hebridean sky
many blued, clouds shadowed
almost purple, ready to weep
for the colour
of an artist's longing.

The bluest of blues
comes from beyond
the seas.
Renoir took it to celebrate
La Parisienne
and Titian
the purity of the Virgin's robes.

The distant blue
is childhood's remembered hills,
my blue heaven.

Seen from space
the Earth is blue

and underfoot
the colour will fade
with the dying
bluebells.

Gentians that grow
on a famine road

can't be told,
the colour won't hold.

It's a story handwritten
in washable ink.

Indigo

is the Hebridean sea, around rocks,
where it isn't turquoise.
It's the deep skies
of a Jolomo painting.

Louis Marcoussis used Indigo
to make the space beyond
the open door, and the rhythm
of the background sea.

Indigo is the glowing polish
of aubergines and the shine
of Renoir's wet umbrellas.

It's inky writing,
a once upon a time story
from over the seas,
and the exotic usurper
of home-grown woad.

Indigo is a dark memory
of starving peasants
in Bengal and Bihar
forced out of food growing

to make the colour
of a bruise, a tragedy,
threatening clouds
in a summer sky.

Violet

Shadow colour
the opposite of light
complementing yellow.

A mourning colour
'Sad and ailing,' Kandinsky said

but Monet saw
fresh air as violet.

I wonder, did he sense
ultraviolet light?

Christopher Wood sought
a perfect shade of violet
to show the depth
of the sea's mystery.

While Winifred Nicholson's *Two Agapanthus*
have a lightly violet touch
which is also a far away longing
in *Blue Mountain Flowers.*

Violet is silky and secretive
blushing damson dark
amongst the late summer leaves.

Violet is the deep purple
of Cleopatra's sails*,

beloved of songbirds and honey bees
yet hardly noticed.

It's the last colour
on the rainbow spectrum,
ending the known,
beginning the unknown,
calling to something beyond itself –

something between the rainbow
and its secretive echo.

---

* Antony and Cleopatra, William Shakespeare, II.2

from
Words and Wonderings
2011

The words and wonderings of being alive

I am thankful for:
insights that show me straight lines are overrated,
logic and reason don't solve everything,
the table is round
and there's music in the air;
quiet moments, noisy moments, inspiring moments;
voices that echo in my mind
and become friends;
all-sorted conversations;
seeds that don't stay
where they are put;
my friend's shoes that encourage walking on air
which is not an element for walking on;
earth-supported, water-washed, air-blessed, fire-inspired
bread and poetry;
people who in all their extraordinary ordinariness
turn up on the doorstep like parcels
of wonderful surprises;
connections and process;
being and becoming;
today and tomorrow which are different
and always will be.

Might it be called wisdom?

It's as we approach old age,
I think, that we see at last
the loveliness of things
once overlooked.
There are moments
minor epiphanies
not remarkable in themselves
that lodge in the memory
to be recalled long afterwards.

And still I know neither where I am
nor why

nor does it matter.

Bread poetry

Late summer sunlight
on the floor of the forest:
dead wood, fungus, damp earth
yeast – this is where we make
our bread and shape
our words.

Bread is the form
of my poem:
seed, flour, dough
in my hand
shape and expression
the rhythm of the loaf.

Bread broken: taste
on my tongue,
grain in my mouth –
the poetry of my being:
beauty of all
our beginnings
earth, food, word.

If

If I am always surprised:
at the intricacy
of the smallest flower,
the fragility of a grain
of wheat,
the eternal light
in the eyes of a child,
the unspoken story
in the lines and folds
on an old woman's skin,

the way each year
the beech leaves
unfurl in spring
with colour that is beyond
any description of green,
and a dandelion
might some days
outshine the sun

If I walk the making,
the celebration
and allow myself
to be shaped by the sound
of the wind
and coloured by a slant
of sunlight

If I look into another's eyes
and see a life fully lived
in moments unremarkable
but lodged in the memory:
a story that is other
than mine yet is also mine

If I greet each day
knowing that what happens
is the chance that something
might

If I begin to grope towards
what can't be told
but can be shared

then I can begin to feel
that beauty will save the world
and know that I am
alive.

Pomegranates

The sun was gentler then,
warm on the bricks
of the back step
where we sat
feasting on pomegranates,
the juice running crimson
down our chins
We bit unceremoniously
into the fruit,
not recognising the gift,
then picked out seed
after seed, innocently
devouring our childhood.

What I know about orchards …

… is that they test the seasons
with frankness:
flaunting blossom
dropping fruit
feeding wild things.

They make life better:
I may be comforted
by little ordered groves
neither field
nor woodland;
neither place to hunt
nor place to gather
but place to be.

Orchards are part of a pattern
we make for ourselves:
hedgerows, hills, houses
picnics and pies,

symbols, festivals, legends
songs and stories.
There are voices in the trees
and you can hear apples fall
long after the tree stops fruiting.

Apple trees are magic.

You can't not look
at an orchard in bloom.

Conversation

Shall we talk of God
you and I, or shall we leave
G-O-D and make
this word of countless mysteries
a window
on to the processes
of relationship and being,
of the pull of memory
and the light of prophecy,
of opening arms
and coming home?

A dream of markets …

that are sensual
not abstract

and smell of flesh, growing things,
warm animals, sun on coloured awnings,
never to be forgotten scents
of strawberries, new bread, fresh coffee.

Such markets are coloured
by every shade of vegetable, fruit
 … and people …

who know themselves
beyond their working
days, bigger
than their achievements.

People with baskets
to carry their needs
and voices to tell
their stories:

knowing, with clowns and poets,
that here is a window to look out
on our own place. Here, where people meet
and sing again, buying and selling
is always aligned to the heart's growth.

The seas of Kirk Swarf *

A composer on the shore
walking the music,
tuning in to the tide

and the rhythm
of moon and sun,
wind and waves.

A wild sea from Westray
and a calm sea from the east,

a glimpse of light
between islands.

A chapel on the shore;
a morning of undreamt truths,
shifting sounds, new-washed
as the world's beginning.

Music comes, music goes.
He meets his own footprints
in the sand like notes
of a score:

a vision that soars
like the sea eagle
into air so clear
it defines thought

like birth or death.

* Stretch of sea off the Holmes of Ire, Sanday, Orkney and a small concerto for bass clarinet and string orchestra by Sir Peter Maxwell Davies.

Symphony

Sounds arranged on a stave of light:
an artist's responsibility.
A process towards
what can't be told
any other way –
a story of beauty
that will save the world.

A good story
that doesn't need me.

Waiting for an artist

Glimpsed in passing:
empty chair and open books,
sunlight touching the room,
oystercatchers on the shore,
the sea beyond,
flowers in the window,

a place to know and meet
and sing again.

A poem to saunter with …

... to gather fragments – the ruins
of a nunnery, or pieces
of Sappho, or the beginnings
of a wall I saw once
on the island: piles of stones,
awaiting their remaking
into a whole, held in time
ready to protect the vulnerable,
the way words are held
by semi-colons, staging posts
on the journey
the mind makes day
after day – a grace
of memory.

The music of humanity
(a celebration of the West-Eastern Divan Orchestra)

Listen. Listen each to each.
This is me. This is you,
occupied and occupier –
this is us in a story
not yet our own.
We move with passion
towards perfect sound
and absolute commitment.
All voices equally responsible
for the beauty of the moment,
all equal before the music:
before Beethoven and Brahms,
before Schubert and Elgar.

True and effortless spirit,
creativity and humanity,
is the logic of the world
of music making possible:
an Egyptian oboist's solo
with Israelis in support;
an Israeli flute solo
with Arabs in support.

An image for justice.
A story of peace.

In a notebook

of handmade paper
I will save

the wide sky sounds
in my mother's voice.

Alasdair's wonder
at the downy newness
of beech leaves.

Apple trees that grow
amongst the trees
of the forest.

A pomegranate,
apple of seeds,
that reminds me of sunlight
on the back step
of my childhood home.

The way light is
between islands,
the white sound of wind,
the willow colour of a whisper,
a small posy on a coffin,
the presence of angels.

A spider called Spurious

He was named by a poet
and lives out of reach
among rafters and crossbeams,
a nomad of sorts
wandering the strokes, the struts
and the purlins.

I imagine at night he comes down
and walks the words on the poet's page
as if he were crossing a field
full of flowers. Knapweed and daisies,
or grass-heads and buttercups,
the shapes are all there.
Letter by letter, he walks
softly over the story of life.

He leaves little sign of his passing by.
He's one of earth's small things –
a detail – and could be anywhere
like a feeling in waiting,
untold and unwritten.

He goes back to his place
between king post and collar beam,
just visible, silent, tantalising,
knowing what he knows.

Communing

The harmony may be impossible
and the melody difficult.
The story is of a disorderly god
whose ways are disturbance
and compromise.

The poet, unable to deny miracles,
continually dreams
dreams which have the fragrance
of precious oil poured out
to soothe away the world's hurt.

This private agony will always seek
a louder song, to sing
in the world's ear, and comfort
those unseen; a song
that will never drown sensitivity
to preserve sanity, a song that moves
towards the hope
that the final note
is joy.

Hope: a moment of being

As if the word is 'Yes'
as if there were light
at the end of the tunnel,
as if there were good
to be illuminated.

An affirmation
that the tinsel
will never outshine
the sunlight

and yesterday will be valued
as if there will be tomorrow
and it will be good.

The fire, the circle, the listening, the talking

Where we come from,
where we belong,
how to live and maybe
how to die – stories
shaped from our being.
A pilgrimage through language
movement by precious movement.
The memories written in tears
on long-loved faces,
shaped in the movement
of hands worn by the world,
or sad in the watery depth
of eyes weary of the search.

These tell the world
an atom at a time.

In the garden

One with colour and creation,
growth and blossoming,
we think we know
how the garden will grow.
We ponder naming and nature
with trowels and forks
spade and rakes,

setting the seeds
that hold our dreams,
quietly growing words,
carrying stories in baskets.

We cover the holes in life
with sunflowers
and forget-me-nots.

A few strangely sweet hours
in a particular place
that might hold all things

collecting, cultivating, conserving
the homely acts of earth-keeping.

The story

I see how you are shaped
and made by wind and starlight.
Winged words tell dreams
and memories, fear
and the sense of loss
that pulls us after it.

Language is thought.
Thought is words
that are always
making and remaking –
the poem that is your life
and mine too:

how we move to tears
that tell the story
more loudly than words;

how we move
towards last things
towards the mindfulness
of silence.

from
A Way of Knowing
2012

A way of knowing

The heightened colours
in an ordinary room
where a child sleeps,
empty bowls on the table,
a turning dial
on a washing machine,
the old man who waits
for tomorrow's sun,
the star that fell from an envelope
my grandsons gave me at Christmas,
cabbages in an organic garden,
lights in my neighbour's window,
gannets over the sea,
dolphins in the sound
on a day of delight,
a boat under a tarpaulin,
the words of a prayer
taken out of the ordinary
run of language,
a pile of stones, waiting
like the words of a poem
for the hands
that will guide them,
the lasting colour
of birch leaves
at the end of autumn,
the handful of seeds

and the mouthful of bread
that make despair impossible.

A way of being and placing,
seeing and naming,

that holds the intensity
of the moment,
cherishing it,

playing the music of dailyness
through all remembering:
a way to the intelligence
of the heart.

Poetry

like the flight of a bird
caught in the sunlight
then disappearing into the trees:
something seen and re-created
made known
for always

Wild places

There is hope
beyond measure
in the way small boys
turn over dead wood
to see worms and beetles:
to know the half hidden
world of small things

What I know about Orkney is that …

… the story and poetry
of all experience
continually colours
my perceptions;

… the sea lapping
at life's edge
can be seen
almost everywhere

and where you can't see it
you know it's there
just over the hill;

... the isle is full of music,
wave roll, bird cry,
wind in the grass,
wind over rock,
wind made solid
by its ever-presence;

 ... larks and curlews
soar and sing
the whole summer night;

 ... sometimes silences are planted
on bare hillsides and blossom
into the wordless stories
of gardens;

... two tone weathering sandstone
sculptured by wind and rain,
and uncanny light
make St Magnus Cathedral
a people's place,
a homecoming beyond home
in music, memory
and centring story.

Scissors

Cold to my touch,
the metal almost black
and rusted in places,
the centre bolt worn smooth:
they carry their age
with style.

There's a maker's mark
I can't quite read
but I can see 'Norwich'
where the story began,
around 1924 when my mother,
at just fourteen, began work
in a shoe factory.

They helped her cut free
from the bonds of service,
stayed with her into adult life,
possibly the only thing
she owned in her childhood,
and a reminder of the ever-present
possibility of poverty.

They were used all the years
of my childhood, their place
never taken by a new pair
and they held on to their secret
until just before she died.

Then they came to me
with their enduring story
of a changing world,
and a cutting-edge dream.

Hanging out the words

A memory of Mondays:
Mum stirring up cleanliness
with a bleached stick
creating a rhythm
of hiss and flap and slop,
steam and sweat and shiny faces,
water and soap rainbows.

Then the lines: patterns
of sleeves and legs,
shorts and little dresses,
matching pants and lace-edged vests,
shirts, sheets and socks,
petticoats and pillow cases,
jumpers and skirts.
They are the bunting of the days
of our working and playing,
the flags of our loyalty and loving,
the procession of our lives
hanging out to dry.

They make a story
that won't be untold:
when someone dies
the wearer's smell
doesn't wash out.

Today my washing
won't be dry by dusk.
The days are golden
but getting shorter
and slower. I am reading
between lines of clothes.
The sun is losing power.
I'm beginning to feel cold.

The boat

Begin with the boat,
a thing so small,
thirsty and waiting.
Sun sets on its worn wood.
The possibility of moonlight
floods its gaps.

Whether there is too much
or too little boat depends
on the depths
of my imagination.

Not the splash of the oars
nor the turn of the tiller
but dolphins, gannets
and the magic
a child sees
in the bow wave
will guide me far enough out
to lay the oars on my knees,

to wait, filled with the rowan tree
and the hope of walking a field
on another shore, wait alone
in the no-looking-back quiet
for a whisper of wind
to blow the boat far off.

A grain of sand

In the intricate dance
of earth, air, fire, water
a grain of sand,
waiting on life.

A lifted, moving, making
grain, carrying unseen,
for the whole world,
a burden of microbes

from Sahara desert,
to Amazon rainforest.

Billions of nutrients,
from poor to rich

to encourage seeding,
to promise growth.

How great the beauty
of this interdependence.
Without deserts, no forests:
a speck of thought
that can never again
be too small to matter.

Notes:
Sometime between 1801 and 1805 William Blake wrote, in *Auguries of Innocence:*
> *To see a World in a Grain of Sand*
> *And a Heaven in a Wild Flower,*
> *Hold Infinity in the palm of your hand*
> *And Eternity in an hour.*

In 2010 scientists discovered that for thousands of years nutrients have been carried on Saharan dust to the rainforests of the Amazon.

What I know about flowers

is a tenderness of colours
that makes my heart leap.

They lead me to an understanding
beyond their names and details.

Placed in a vase by a window
they make one revealing surprise
of the very near and the very far,
the tangible and the intangible,
the small and the vast,

and the merest suggestion
of that middle distance
which my eyes leap over.

There is something humbling
about the intensity of blue
in the details of a bluebell
or the vastness of the sky,
the concentration of yellow:
a buttercup in full flower
or the beam of the sun.

If you don't feel
the colour and the light
the looking becomes nothing.

The painterly joy of colour
might be revealed
by one who knows quiet flowers.
Butterwort or bogbean,
dusky cranesbill or daffodils
might light a room.

No beginning, no ending
just awakening.

Poet in the gallery
Simon Armitage reading at the Pier Art Gallery, Stromness

Words settle in the space between,
wash over Shell and Pebble*,
Shellmoon* Goddess ship*;
8 Sceptres*, Fields About Me*,
First Light** and Skimmer.**

The shape of each sound
is as solid as carved wood or stone
and yet as soft as a child's hand
reaching out from far away
to touch a poet's tears.

Words carved out in the silence,
and given frail existence
live on eternally.

They touch the edge
of perception,
showing the way
to what is always
unsaid.

* Sculptures by Frances Pelly
** Sculptures by John Cumming

String Trio, Peter Maxwell Davies
Monday 23rd June 2008

The quickness of a reel
gently woven through a slow air.
Harmonies moving into places
where they don't usually go

and meeting with presences
comfortable and profound
in their power to discomfort.

Afterwards all thoughtfulness
turns to the remains
of pure sound

and the rhythm of muscles,
the movement of line

that is a composer's smile
reaching beyond a cathedral
full of voices to the depths
of silence.

Ordinary, particular, universal

What do worship, miracle, praise mean
if not seeing as if for the first time
the particular way evening sunlight
touches the edge of the garden

or waiting on a day
of great delight
to see dolphins

or the sustaining memories
brought back to my mother
as she held in her arms
her first great grandson

or at the end of a week
of conversation, celebration, challenge
walking together, old friends,
the three of us in the sun
towards the sand and the sea
at the edge of the island –
alive to each
particular joy

wordlessly knowing

the way things are.

from
Glimpsed in Passing
2014

Today ...

... I'll try to make peace
in practice and poetry.
I'll choose words and images carefully,
avoiding all that proscribes, restricts,
oppresses, destroys, humiliates,
patronises, demonises or enslaves.

I'll try to use words
that open minds,
widen moral vision
and motivate the will,
words that show an alternative
to famine, war, racism,
torture and violence,
unjust structures, systems
and relationships.

I may talk about sex
or about violence
but I will resist the media urge
to conflate the two.

I'll not abandon reason
but I'll ask questions
that challenge the relentless
course of logic.

I'll value imagination, story
and poetry that show

there is another way.

I'll fight no fights, not even 'good' ones.
I'll not stand up for Jesus
    or be a soldier of anything
    not even the cross;
    nor wave any flaming swords;
I'll address no one as Lord
    or mighty conqueror
    or put on any sort of armour
    not even the armour of Christ
    or the dressings of power.
I'll not march for Jesus
    or anyone else.
I'll parade no nationalistic flags,
    nor bang any triumphalist drums.
I'll be a pilgrim
and try to walk lightly
for the sake of the earth,
and the diversity of life
it sustains.

I'll recognise the fragility
and finite nature of the earth,
our only home, and resist creatively
all that denies fullness of life by:
    playing, laughing and dancing
    planting trees and sowing seeds
    making and sharing bread

... and ice cream!
lighting candles,
being alive to song and symbol.

I'll look more
and listen more.
I'll live more moments
as given moments.
I'll make this day,
and every day,
a holy day;

I shall make mistakes
and admit to them humbly.

Today I'll dream –
of all sorts of people together,
loving, sharing, playing, dancing
celebrating difference.

And at the end of the day
when things are much the same
I'll continue to hope.
I'll remember that the personal
is always political; that inner peace
cannot be separated from wholeness
and health in community;
that small acts of beauty
by small groups of people
still carry the potential
to change the world.

Wool, wood, stone
Ardalanish Beach
(for Jan)

The windswept beach
where we collect wood
is loud with possibilities.

Cloudshaped woolmakers
float on the hills.
Row on row they work
on the intricate patterns
of landscape.

A rock with the presence
of a Ronald Rae sculpture
is a wind-worn, sea-washed
testament, loud
in its silence.

The evening will be filled
with warm dreams
and the wood-fire whispering
of household gods.

A grey day

Uncertain of the future but free
to allow the sorrows and joys
of lost experience to be reclaimed
and redeemed with words
as yet unborn, I see what must be said
illuminated by its own light only.

In the joy of connections
I come to know
the power of hope
which is beyond my perception
of happiness.

Alone …

… in a cloud-darkened churchyard
I sit unnaturally still, wanting
the almost unbearable to be changed

into something tolerable.
There's no consolation
in reason, mind fails

to ease the turbulence
which is quiet only
in connections, in the closeness

of trees and butterflies,
birds and grass,
and in the wonder of knowing
as the sun breaks through:
all life is here
and it is good.

Big words
(for Steve)

Write the words big
then you'll begin to see
their hidden life,
what it means
to shape letterforms,
and make memory lovely,
to reveal possibilities beyond
naming, to understand maybe
the shapes and colours,
the little bits of imagery
that might touch meaning,
to see the way all things belong
to all other things.

Small writing, small talk
may fill up silence with nothing
but a word will always be more than

itself – like a hand held out
in the darkness, or the movement
of a moment that becomes the way
the earth turns.

Write the words big
you told me, release them
while they still have energy,
and something
will happen.

A photograph of birdsong?
(for Anne who planted the thought)

Isn't it always blue? When I see the sky
and carpets of bluebells, don't they sound
like birds in spring, woods come alive?

Is it ever possible to take a silent photograph
of the woods in the first breath of warm air?
When the call of this year's first cuckoo
echoed across the fields at Easter
wasn't that the sound of fresh leaves
against blue, and the nutty scent
of awakening beech trees?

The gate ...

... fills a gap in a fence
that may one day be a hedge.
One side is home,
the other the whole world.
The gate is a stepping off place
that keeps little in or out.
Badgers come under.
Squirrels come over.
Rabbits are rare visitors
and I've yet to see a deer
come near the gate.

Wind and water easily
breach its defences.
It doesn't divide or control
but joins cut and garden grass
with wild and wind-waving seedheads:
green to green
earth to earth
dust to dust ...

The smell of summer grass
isn't confined to any one side
of a gate that is but an interruption
in the air like the threshold
from life to death.

Glimpsed in passing ...

*What is the opposite
of a boat adrift ...*

It's the way it's always been:
to reach the sea, to stand
watching, waiting; to know
that nothing can be unravelled
to its core

but is like reflecting
where wild flowers
gathered in a vase, framed
by a shore cottage window
make of themselves
a sea-wide subject:
the beauty
of things together.

A blackbird sings
and the song echoes
in fragments of memory.

A choir, unison
of sound,
and a thought
in the wind
the music
of non-oppression.

The first daffodil opens
in the way daffodils do
each spring: fragile
expected, known.

Cuckoo returning
a joy in the tragedy
of the world.

What awaits us
on the other side
of silence
might be an ecstasy
of free-flowing movement
melted and released
by a flame
we learn to see
burning in every bush.

Hold the seed gently.
Know you are holding
a field of wheat,
a loaf of bread,
food with friends
the joy of sharing.

A story re-told.
Five thousand fed on a hillside
and a memory resurrected:
power cut darkness

on the road before dawn,
candles in a window,
porridge and coffee,
a warm fire and friendship.

A sense of beauty, rooted
in human hearts, sharing
the looking and the loving
that makes a sacrament
of everyday experience.

*Resurrection is living
more than ...*

To imagine ...

... a time in the boat,
rowing close to the safety
of the shore yet aware of its distance
reveals the need to pause,
to rest the oars on my knees.
Not to look down
but out to the far horizon,
up to the sky, to be still
and remain one small part
of the bigger picture.

I do not know God

but I do know:
  wind in the treetops
  and the sound of the sea
  as it reaches the shore;
I do know:
  the loveliness of laughter,
  the smell of a baby's head,
  the trust in a child's touch,
  the light in an old woman's eyes,
  hope in a kiss.
I do know:
  music coming from
  and leading to
  silence;
  words on a page –
  story and poetry
  connecting heart and mind,
  thought and imagination.
I do know:
  the mystery of colour
  in an artist's palette
  and the way the potter's hands
  shape the clay.

I do not know God
but I do know:
  leaf mould and lichen,

wood rot and fungi,
new shoots and unfurling leaves,
soil and soul,
death and renewal;
I do know:
ripening wheat
rising dough
and sharing bread;

I do not know God
but I do know:
worms, bees and butterflies,
pattern, change and movement,
fragility and vulnerability;
I do know:
the surprise of strawberries,
the wonder of apples,
and that there is beauty
in a cancer cell magnified.
I do know:
morning sunlight
as it touches
each blade of grass;
the flicker of the smallest flame
and the furthest star

I do not know God
but I do know:
the kindness

   of cleaners and wisdom
   in unexpected places;
I do know:
   that energy and love,
   vision and discernment
   make possibilities
   endless
I do know:
   suffering and joy
   darkness and light
   as integral to being
   fully alive.

I do not know God
but I do know
   that the teachings of Jesus
   are being lived out,
   if not by the church,
   then by grassroots movements
   everywhere.
I do know
   of small groups of people
   making and mending,
   working and wondering,
   growing and sharing,
   meeting and striving,
   questioning and protesting,
   living and loving
   together.

I do not know God
but I do know:
  that the intensity of love
  can be creative
  or destructive.
I do know:
  that defining goodness
  is difficult, if not impossible
  but we know a good person
  when we meet one.

I do not know God
but I do know
  that beauty is gratuitous
  and peace, beyond certainty
  or purpose, is in the knowing
  and the unknowing.

A time to walk … and a time to stand …
(For Jan)

Blackberries in a borrowed milk can,
driftwood collected in a Co-op bag,
elderberries and mushrooms,
hazelnuts and sloes,
hips and crabapples.

All the world
was once wild like this
and life for looking,
seeing and gathering
the fruits of moments:
the bird in the tree,
the morning light,
the first daffodil,
spring blowing through
the ruins of winter,
the smell of summer grass,
children's laughter,
an apple and a tree
in Milton's garden,
the do-not-disturb wonder
of our knowing
time is nothing
but the running down
of clock weights
and the swing
of the pendulum.

Speed is violence.

Go home slowly carrying your excuses
for being where you have been!

On the earth
(for Anne)

When you're on dry soil
and the rain comes
and the scent
is as if it runs
from the veins of the gods
don't look up
to the sky
for the miracle.
Look at your feet
at the earth
you walk on.
From there are springing
nothing but miracles:
the roots, the beginnings,
the little flowers
that are what life
at its best consists of.

Smell and look and know.
Wonder in the silence
at paradise unspoken
for it's this wonder
that makes you
a human being
fully alive.

Note

There is a word for rain on the dry earth: *petrichor* derived from petra/stone and –ichor/the fluid that flows in the veins of the gods in Greek mythology.

A workaday fiddle ...

... a modest instrument
tough enough to travel
the Arctic silence in a kayak
and well suited to an owner*
who knew where to learn
the secrets of survival.

Black paint almost worn away
by fingers low down
in the fiddling position –

tells a story of Scottish reels
in the cold, cold air
of remote trading posts;

tells of dancing feet;
tells as clearly
as a worn floor;

tells about the people's longing
for curlew calls, oystercatcher cries
and the songs of home.

Silent, behind museum glass
it holds its story,
keeps its memory magic,
waits to speak of home
to wanderers everywhere;
waits for the heart of one man's
almost forgotten story
to be heard again
in the people's music.

* Arctic explorer John Rae. His fiddle, recently restored by Mark Shiner and played by Jennifer Wrigley, is displayed in Stromness Museum.

'The sea wants to be visited'*

Shall we go down to the shore today,
down the path where grass is sweet,
and follow the light to the edge of the bay
past the mill and its chattering stream.

Shall we go down to the shore today,
with our windblown thoughts of waving wheat,
and follow the scents of seaweed and salt
down to where earth and water meet.

Shall we go down to the shore today,
to the place of dreams and ghosts of bread,
to savour the moment and stand at the edge
where time is early and all has been said.

* Gaelic proverb

'A few … may creep back, silent'*

and so he did, my granddad,
back to his wife
and six young daughters,
carrying inside his untold story.

Home and silent,

a man gassed and damaged:
a useless arm, his mind
not quite as it should be
and a fondness for drink.

Home and silent,

they lived with his story
this broken man,

who once made shoes
for a living, then went
reluctantly to war,
and the woman who nurtured
his silence and bore him
another girl, a child with a mind
not quite as it should be.

The words that tell are lost
like those of another story:
my great-uncle who deserted,
was given shelter once,
and never heard of again –

lost in the great silence.

But the energy, the life
and the loving,
stronger than the killing
and the wounding,
bigger than words,
is here in my living,
honouring the silence,
bearing on the body
what I cannot know
and only poetry can tell.

* Wilfred Owen, from *The Send Off*

Abiding (2)

(Bedouin shepherds driven off
ancestral lands by Israeli Defence Force)

If shepherds no longer abide
what will happen to hope,
to the promise of Christmas?
What will happen to the stories
if ordinary people
are no longer able to live
as their spirit leads them?

We all carry some connection
to the story and the stillness,
the waiting in fields,
on hillsides, in homes,
in churches and monasteries.
Suffering prevails
when there is no imagination
and the story remains untold.

If shepherds are driven from their lands
and are no longer abiding, it matters to us.
What happens to one
happens to us all
and in the injustice
we all lose something
of what it means
to be human.

Golden Wedding
13th June, 2014

Knowing
the everyday beauty
of fifty years
of days
in all their detail
and wonder,
knowing
that love is so much more
than when we stood diffident
in the church porch
on our Wedding Day
wanting what was good,
not knowing
what it was –
until now.

The road home

... seems shorter now,
steeper, with more stones,
noisier in places
but mostly silent,
darker sometimes
yet the light at the end
is often very close.
There is still the search –
but not now for meaning
but for beauty.
There are exquisite moments
in unexpected places –
to be old is to see clearer
the loveliness of things.

The end is around a bend
I can't yet see
but it's there
waiting for me
and you
to be ready.

One day, I'll turn that bend
alone and, I hope,
content.

New Poems
2015/16

A parable of being

See how they come:
young and old,
men, women, children,
all living things,
to the sheltering tree
and the possibility of angels.

See how they come:
bare feet on the warm earth,
disturbing the dust of ages,
to the telling place
where the joy of birth
and beginnings is shared
and the colours
of hope imagined:

>for every baby born, a star
>for all life on earth,
>a story and a promise.

See how they come:
to cherish life,
to wonder
at what they know
and what they don't know,
to make the earth sing.

Re-reading Middlemarch at 70

Turning the pages
of an old Penguin,
age-browned, scented
with the years,
I'm feeling again
the desires and dreams
of youth; remembering
the hopes of noble gestures;
then re-connecting
with the reconciliations
of middle age.

Dorothea's vision
might have been mine
when all I could read
was the vision.
How different my perception
now the humour and the pathos
are more knowable.
I laugh and cry
in different places.
I remember my hopes for love
and know now the small acts
of beauty and kindness
that make life bearable,
know the experience
of growing old in love

and what it is
for love to grow old.

I'm on a different level
of knowing, looking back
understanding better, maybe
how a book reads me.

Last leaves

The wind is taking
the last of the leaves,
scattering gold
beneath our feet.

Thinning light comes askance
and catches by surprise
branches and a few seedpods.
The revealed beauty
of the barest trees
suggests absence
yet holds our eyes.

People don't stay out so long.
Rain seems to drown
the memory of sunshine

but a smile is left behind
when they go indoors.

Earth gives off its autumn
scent: the air is quiet.
Shadows move round
as the sun follows its course
and everything settles
to a sense of ripeness
and ending.

On a washed-out winter day
imagination colours our thoughts
and makes us content to wait
for summer leaves to come again,
content to look for quiet surprises
in the rhythm and change
of earth's winter song.

Knitting pattern

Well into the Advent season:
dark days, long nights, life waiting.
Memories bid me one day to seek out
and take from their yellowing tissue
a knitted shawl and christening robe:
work of a long ago Advent
when, like Mary, I waited
for the birth of my firstborn,
waited to wrap him
in the softness of lambswool.

The shawl rests on my arm
like the trace of a web,
tethered to everything.
The wool still smells sweet.
I hold it out to show my friend
the fine work: two-ply for babies, tiny needles,
intricate pattern work learnt from mum.
Even as a small child I knew
how to follow a pattern.

There's peace in the moment,
in the making and now the sharing,
peace-filled, suited to Advent,
to waiting quietly for a child
and pondering things in the heart.

Even now I can smell new babies,
feel the warmth of love and home
where new life would be welcomed
and celebrated, where injustice, oppression,
power and talk of war were resisted
in the simple craft of knitting.

Those knitters at the guillotine
we learnt about as children –
were they resisting too?

Knitting is a nurturing craft
without instant gratification.
I understand its beauty better now:
the hope of preparation;
the love of waiting;
the faith that works
to a different pattern.

Thoughts on doing nothing …

… that it might be creative,
and good dreaming;

… that the good might be
to let action go,
to resist the often destructive
compulsion to *do*;

… that it is movement: the mind
not focused on one thought,
but absorbing surroundings
and wandering freely
through many thoughts;

… that mostly it is waiting,
expecting something or somebody
might happen;

… that it might be the moment
when I feel fully alive;

… that there is beauty, somehow,
to be seen almost everywhere.

Housekeeping
(for Alison)

Bread has been baked this morning
to celebrate your coming
and spinach picked from the garden.
We will know the pleasures
of good food grown, served, shared
in companionship and trust,
in ordinary living,
in living fully.

A bed has been well made
with freshly washed sheets,
dried in the open air,
scented with sunlight and wind.

All things are orderly,
clean and wholesome:
the signs and symbols
of our living are to share.
Things of our life grounded here
are touched with love
and ready to welcome you.

All this might talk itself
into the poetry of domesticity,
the home becoming central;

into the words of women's being:
of nurture, care and staying put,
the language of small things,
and the faithful patterns
of our living.

The ways of the world …
… thoughts in a doctors' waiting room
(for Emily)

She, all of two years old, sociable,
wanting conversation, watches
him across the room.
He, younger, knowing only a few
essential words, thinks, it seems,
something should happen here.
He holds out the fruit
he's enjoying, and tries out
a lovely word: 'apple'.
She's ready for conversation –
it's what people do
and she knows how to do it.
'I'm Isabel. What's your name?'

'Apple,' he responds joyfully –
this is the useful word
that matters to him just now.
She consults his Mummy.
'What's his name?'
'Jacob,' says Mummy.
Isabel is excited now.
She has something to tell
and looks across the room
to a woman waiting at Reception:
'Mummy, he's Jacob,' she calls.
Girl and boy watch each other
in the way children do,
not needing purpose,
not expecting anything.
Then it's time for her to leave
and Jacob, confused a little,
watches the door as she goes out,
watches her go down the road
and disappear in the distance.
He acknowledges she's missing:
'Gone!' he announces to us all,
then continues enjoying his apple.

Spring haiku

As if daffodils
have waited for this moment
to yellow the world.

What does the purple
of the crocus want to say
to the early light?

Summer haiku

Evening light slants
across the silent garden.
Warmed insects rise rejoicing.

Moss greens the tree trunk
at the place it leaves the earth,
reaching for the blue.

Autumn haiku

Morning mist, drizzle,
light gathered in diamond drops
on a spider's web.

Sun breaking through
slowly touching the last leaves
with a farewell kiss.

Winter haiku

In darkness and cold
of heart, reading with new eyes
a long-untouched book.

Sombre winter scene:
the pure joy of emptiness,
the beauty of hope.

Bowl

I may talk of God
or I may hold, for a moment,
this bowl with its blue inside,
with its perfect bowl shape,
perfect, but its unique self.
I may feel the outer roughness,
and see the cave-like drawings,
reminding me of something,
conflicting somehow with perfection.
I see, within, the lines
that show its making:
where human hands have been;
and then the colour, oh the colour:
deep blue of morning and memory,
held in the bowl, contained
but released by my looking.
A sea and sky bowl; a dreamtime thing;
going all places; taking me everywhere
endlessly like a large cup of life
running over.

To laugh …

… is to celebrate good cells,
light the candle at both ends,
make the candle into a bonfire.

To resist the search
for purpose and meaning;
accept that life is, and just be
and be justly.

To laugh …
… is to enjoy sunlight
on a spring morning,
lighting up the primroses,

to know that the gift of life
must be enjoyed when it can be
and misery will not be alleviated
by denying joy.

To laugh …
… is prayer. It is music
in the air, and water running
over stones.

It is living for one moment
as if the future we dream
is already here.

If I am ever thankful

If I am ever thankful
for the life I live

I am showing
that I understand life
as a gift
to be cherished
and any entitlement
to what I might call mine
as an illusion.

If I am ever thankful
for the life I live

the greed that might be
in me and may be in others
could be overcome.

If I am ever thankful
for the life I live

apathy will dissolve into nothing
and responses will become creative.

If I am ever thankful
for the life I live

any tendency to violence
will be overcome by forgiveness,
gentleness and kindness.

*If we are ever thankful
for the lives we live*

we can together overcome fear
and work courageously
for a just and peaceful future.

History

There is a story
in the shape of a tree
that was crafted
once into a hedge
and now grows free;

in the pattern
of stone walls
across wild lands;

in the way the sea
one fateful day reveals,
for a short time,

footprints made in the sand
long years ago
and then washes them away;

in the way one day we see things
in a different light, and know
all life is here in this moment
as wide as the sky,
as deep as the sea,
as precious as the earth.

Shoreline:

the place between that holds
the fragrance of small islands
and the music of memory;

the place of sea change,
of things rich and new,
of the song and the sinew,

of choices: imaginative preferences,
here or there, now or then.

We may pick up a pebble
and never know
if it's been shaped by the sea

or worked by human hands
or maybe both.

The place between tides
belongs to no one
and so is ours for a while
outside time, beyond
our understanding of place.

Thoughts too deep?

Over seventy years of crying
for one sad thing or another
and my eyes are dry
and I have no tears

for the inexpressible hurt
of suffering people,
ravaged lands,
or beauty destroyed
by human greed;

no Ezra howl to challenge
the ways of a broken world,
to lament all we are losing,
to mourn for life gone before
we begin to understand it.

But deep inside,
too deep for tears,
too deep for words,
the river of weeping
flows on

and will flow
beyond my death.

Withdrawn*

There are boats
in the woods
the beautiful woods,
wooden boats, mysterious,
eerie and empty but holding on
to their names:
Gloria Jean, Joanne Marie,
Seahorse, Grey Gull, Martha.
We know who they are
but where did they voyage
before they came to the trees
all out of place and telling of change?

They've a story to tell;
a story in questions.

Where is the sea, the water?

Did it once rise so high
and leave behind the boats,
leave us thinking:
How can this be?

There's a poem in the air,
a song of the sea, of fishermen
fishing where fish are no longer,
and of things in the sea
that shouldn't be there – pollution
of water and woods undervalued.

There's the politics here
that need not be named.
The imagination of ordinary people
is stretched to seek a new story.

And children will come
to boats in the woods.
They know about surprises,
and about big questions.
The answers they seek
will begin this new story
of our finite planet, beautiful,
fragile and needing our care.

* From April to September 2015 a flotilla of five boats, an installation by artist Luke Jerram, nestled among the trees of Leigh Woods above the River Avon, Bristol.

Christmas card angel

There she is, the gentle angel,
a little sentimental maybe,
nostalgic surely. She exists
only in the colourful
depths of our minds
and the fanciful realms
of childhood stories.

But pause a moment
in the winter gloom:
imagine the possibility
of the impossible dream,
hope waiting to be heard,
imaged in this feathered being.

Might the trumpet sound
for a more compassionate world,
a gentler, more harmonious way
where just living brings peace,
where greed is known to be evil,
and sharing is a way of life;
where extremes of wealth
and poverty are history.

May this unreal angel,
the quiet beauty of imagination,
call to fullness of life
all that is real, good
and surprising
at the heart
of our being.

At the Broch of Gurness*

Boys and girls
come out to play
as the sun sets.
They jump from stone
to waiting stone,
run in the shadows
of peoples and homes
yet to be uncovered,
earlier than we know.

I watch, knowing poetry
feeling words
in the air, waiting
to reveal a mystery
as old as the stones,
as new as the children.

What will they uncover
in their play – these young lives
unaware yet respectful
of the ground they tread,
seeming to feel what is part
of their story, knowing
the place their own.

Their voices, gentle and clear,
mingle with the ghosts
of the long dead: a symphony,
a harmony, music and rhythm
diverse but united and endless
as thought and prayer.

*One of a group of structures along the shores of Eynhallow Sound, Orkney Mainland. It dates from around 500BCE, or maybe earlier.

From the edge …

In Iona Abbey
two small images
watch from the back
of the Leader's Chair –
one reads; one prays.

Wooden saint, often unnoticed,
what are the thoughts
that come from your book?
Wooden saint, often forgotten
what are the prayers
behind your closed eyes?

You are inconspicuous art,
silent, always there
behind many loved heads,
above many wise words.

You are guardians of our visions,
holders of our hopes and dreams,
the form of our waiting,
the shape of our longing.

Emptiness

Open moorland, a place of sombre beauty
not accepted landscape, or picturesque.

A space that needs time
for looking closely,
to discover the power
of the moment
in tiny flowers and creatures
unseen at distance;
to live in the now
of the small and immediate.

Winter: prospect drained of colour
yet filled with the beauty of form
and anticipation of future joys.

Then: at the end
of all expectancy,
to accept the gathering
and the letting go
of all things
in the now of death,
moment of silence,
moment of transformation
into peace and love.

To be called Joy

Sunlight on the year's new leaves
early in the morning;
a dragonfly coming to rest
on my shoulder, staying, unafraid;
a passing butterfly:
glimpse of inexpressible colour;
the robin eating from my hand
and the blackbird's song again.
Then intensity of light everywhere
as I leave the hospital
after the cancer diagnosis.

These I trust without question
and know joy is to connect
with all vulnerable life forms.

And maybe to be called Joy
is a unique gladness, reminder
of transience of being,
delight unbounded
and obligation to enjoy.

Wild Goose Publications is part of the Iona Community:

- An ecumenical movement of men and women from different walks of life and different traditions in the Christian church
- Committed to the gospel of Jesus Christ, and to following where that leads, even into the unknown
- Engaged together, and with people of goodwill across the world, in acting, reflecting and praying for justice, peace and the integrity of creation
- Convinced that the inclusive community we seek must be embodied in the community we practise

Together with our staff, we are responsible for:

- Our islands residential centres of Iona Abbey, the MacLeod Centre on Iona, and Camas Adventure Centre on the Ross of Mull

and in Glasgow:
- The administration of the Community
- Our work with young people
- Our publishing house, Wild Goose Publications
- Our association in the revitalising of worship with the Wild Goose Resource Group

The Iona Community was founded in Glasgow in 1938 by George MacLeod, minister, visionary and prophetic witness for peace, in the context of the poverty and despair of the Depression. Its original task of rebuilding the monastic ruins of Iona Abbey became a sign of hopeful rebuilding of community in Scotland and beyond. Today, we are about 250 Members, mostly in Britain, and 1500 Associate Members, with 1400 Friends worldwide. Together and apart, 'we follow the light we have, and pray for more light'.

For information on the Iona Community contact:
The Iona Community, 21 Carlton Court, Glasgow G5 9JP, UK
Phone: 0141 429 7281
e-mail: admin@iona.org.uk; web: www.iona.org.uk

For enquiries about visiting Iona, please contact:
Iona Abbey, Isle of Iona, Argyll PA76 6SN, UK. Phone: 01681 700404
e-mail: ionacomm@iona.org.uk

Wild Goose Publications, the publishing house of the Iona Community established in the Celtic Christian tradition of Saint Columba, produces books, e-books, CDs and digital downloads on:

- holistic spirituality
- social justice
- political and peace issues
- healing
- innovative approaches to worship
- song in worship, including the work of the Wild Goose Resource Group
- material for meditation and reflection

For more information:

Wild Goose Publications
The Iona Community
21 Carlton Court, Glasgow, G5 9JP, UK

Tel. +44 (0)141 429 7281
e-mail: admin@ionabooks.com

or visit our website at
www.ionabooks.com
for details of all our products and online sales